This book Belongs to:

_____

In memory of:

_____

To Jack. In memory of Maya. -BM

To my treasured siblings in heaven and on earth. -AL

Copyright 2022 Bella Mody
Illustrated by Anna Lindgren
ISBN 979-8-9856671-1-0 (paperback)
979-8-9856671-0-3 (hard cover)
979-8-9856671-2-7 (Ebook)

All rights reserved. No part of this publication may be reproduced, distributed, or transmitted in any form or by any means, including photocopying, recording, other electronic or mechanical methods, or by any information storage and retrieval system now known or hereafter invented, without the prior written permission of the publisher, except in the case of brief quotations embodied in critical reviews and certian other noncommercial uses permitted by copyright law. For permission requests, contact the Maya's Wings Foundation at info@themayaswingsfoundation.org
For bulk or wholesale ordering, contact the author: Bella@themayaswingsfoundation.org
Visit us on the web! www.themayaswingsfoundation.org

I am a big brother.
My sister, she died. I picture her with wings.

I imagine her flying in the sky while I ride my bike.
I tell her everything.

I tell her about the wildflowers and pick one for her too.

I tell her about my favorite sports and the animals at the zoo.

I teach my sister about my world, the things I see and hear. Like ice cream trucks outside the park and music in my ears.

She teaches me to close my eyes and enjoy the smell of air.

To trust the things I cannot see but know that they are there.

I love my baby sister, even though we never met.

Mom says that she loved me too.
She looked like me, I bet.

Mom was sad the day my sister died, and wings grew on her back. But I knew I had a job to do, and I would do just that.

Some big brothers help change diapers, some play peek-a-boo.

Sometimes I feel sad because my sister is not here.

I have a big important job that I know I can do.
Because I am brave, strong and kind;
and my hugs are special too.

To give the wind a great big hug and feel my sister by my side.

Note from the Author

To the older brother or sister reading this book:

You are the best that you can be, and this is clear for all to see. After a brother or sister dies, some days are more challenging than others. I know it isn't fair that your baby brother or sister is not here physically with you today. It is OK to feel sad, angry, worried, or any other feeling you may have. Your grownups, friends, and family can all help you with these big feelings, and the good feelings too. The connection you have with your baby brother or sister is so unique that it lights up the world around you. Keep shining your light, even when it wants to fade; and know that you are loved. That will never change. Love does not end when a loved one dies. Love stays with you forever, and can be felt all around you, as sure as each sunrise, and as strong as the wind.

To the parents reading this book:

I hold you in my heart as we navigate the unimaginable and duality of grief that is the loss of a child, as well as the loss of the life we had imagined for our family.

There is no word to describe a parent who has lost a child; nor is there a word to describe the child who has lost a sibling. I encourage you to give yourself permission to have days to not feel okay, remember to take care of yourself, honour those around you and their individual healing process, and grant your living children the same permissions. I see your grief and encourage you to see theirs. It is my hope that this book can spark the start of many conversations and connections to help you and your little ones receive the healing you deserve.

Bella Mody is a physical therapist, educator, wife and mama. She is an activist who is passionate about equity in healthcare. She is the bereaved mother of her sweet daughter, Maya, and the proud founder of The Maya's Wings Foundation. She lives in Portland, Oregon with her wife, Maya's big brother, and their three dogs.
Learn more at www.themayaswingsfoundation.org

Anna lindgren is an older sibling to her departed angel sister, Gabriel. She resides in Grand Rapids, Michigan with her growing family and is dedicated to sharing her art through murals, custom paintings and book illustrations. Anna has spent years teaching art in hopes to inspire others to discover the passion of making beautiful things.
More of her work may be viewed at www.annasartavenue.com

CPSIA information can be obtained
at www.ICGtesting.com
Printed in the USA
BVHW060856300323
661445BV00003B/73